# Take-Home Books
## Grade 1

**Harcourt**

Orlando   Boston   Dallas   Chicago   San Diego

Visit *The Learning Site!*
**www.harcourtschool.com**

Copyright © by Harcourt, Inc.

All rights reserved. No part of this publication may be reproduced or transmitted in any form or by any means, electronic or mechanical, including photocopy, recording, or any information storage and retrieval system.

Teachers using COLLECTIONS may photocopy complete pages in sufficient quantities for classroom use only and not for resale.

HARCOURT and the Harcourt Logo are trademarks of Harcourt, Inc.
Printed in the United States of America

ISBN 0-15-317812-4

3 4 5 6 7 8 9 10   054   2003 2002 2001 2000

# Contents

TAKE-HOME BOOK
**Together Again**
Use with "A Big Surprise."

# The Big House

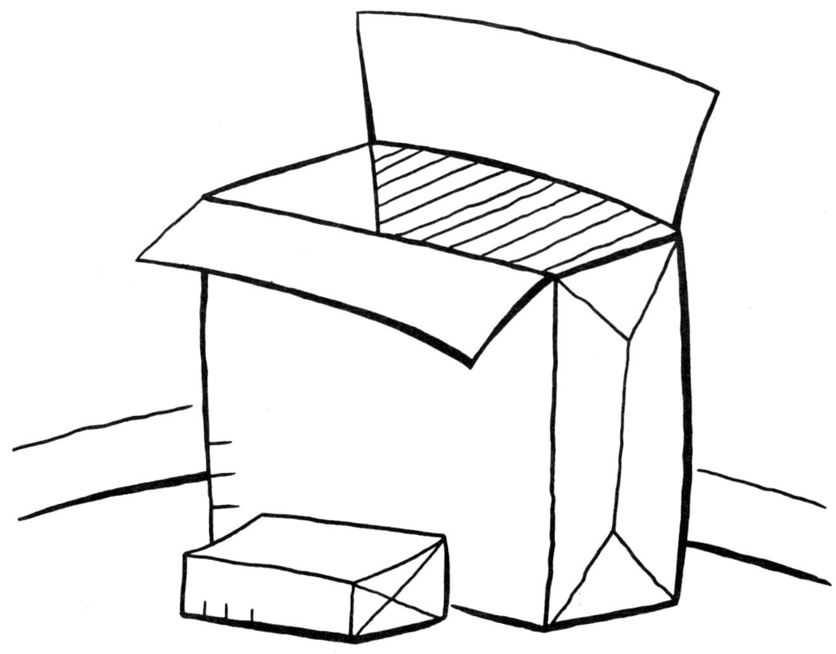

## by Lynn Trepicchio
## illustrated by Jackie Snider

## Teacher/Family Member .................................................

### My Box

Have children draw a picture of a box—like the one in the story—showing who would live in it. Ask children to describe the activities they would use the box for.

 **School-Home Connection**

Invite your child to read aloud *The Big Box.* Help him or her read the animal names in the story.

Word Count:            34

Vocabulary Words:      big
                       here
                       house
                       is
                       the
                       what

Phonic Elements:       Consonants: /m/ *m*, /s/ *s*; Short Vowel: /a/ *a*

What a big house!

Here is a box.

Here is the big box.

Here is the big box.

Here is the dog.

Here is the mouse.

Here is the frog.

Here is the cat.

TAKE-HOME BOOK
**Together Again**
Use with "Come Here, Tiger"

# Where Is Sam?

by Ruby Mae

illustrated by Jesse Clay

## Teacher/Family Member ..........................................

### Warm/Cold Game

Have your child choose an object in the room for you to find. Stand in the middle of the room and, as you move around the room searching for the object, have your child tell you if you are getting "warmer" (closer) or "colder" (farther away) until you find the object.

 **School-Home Connection**

Invite your child to read aloud *Where Is Sam*? Help him or her find and read all of the vocabulary words in the story.

Word Count: 30

Vocabulary Words:
are
come
in
look
that
where
you

Phonic Elements: Consonants: /t/ *t*, /k/ *c*

Harcourt

Here I am!

Where is Sam?

Where are you, Sam?

Here you are!

Where is that Sam?

Come look in here.

Where are you, Sam?

Come look in the hat.

Harcourt

TAKE-HOME BOOK
*Together Again*
Use with "Look at Me."

# We Are Big Now

## by Robert Fletcher
## illustrated by Neil Posis

## Teacher/Family Member...........................................

### I Am Big Now

With your child, make a list of all of the things he or she can do now.
Continue to add to the list during the school year.

 **School-Home Connection**

Invite your child to read aloud *We Are Big Now*. Make flash cards for all
the vocabulary words and review them.

Word Count:            41

Vocabulary Words:      be
                       good
                       hard
                       it
                       me
                       now
                       read
                       run
                       to
                       too
                       we

Phonic Elements:       Consonants: /m/ *m*, /d/ *d*

Harcourt

It is good to be
big now.

8

I am big now.

1

I read to you.

What are you good at?

Now that looks
hard to me!

It is good to read.

I run to you.

It is good to run, too.

TAKE-HOME BOOK
*Together Again*
Use with "I Went Walking."

# The
# Black Dog

by Lynn Trepicchio
illustrated by Neil Posis

## Teacher/Family Member ........................................

### Color Concentration

Make a game with colors and color names. On one set of cards, write the color names. Have children color another set of cards, using the corresponding colors. Spread the cards face down on the table, mix them up, and take turns matching the cards.

 **School-Home Connection**

Invite your child to read aloud *The Black Dog*. Help him or her read the color words in the story.

Word Count:             43

Vocabulary Words:       black
                        brown
                        did
                        green
                        red
                        saw
                        see
                        walking
                        went
                        yellow

Phonic Elements:        Consonant:/d/ *d*; Short Vowel:/i/ *i*
                        did

Harcourt

I see a black dog
walking to me!

I went walking.

Did you see a black dog?

I saw a brown dog.

I saw a red dog.

I saw a yellow dog.

Did you see a black dog?

I saw a green dog.

Harcourt

TAKE-HOME BOOK
*Together Again*
Use with "Big Pig and Little Pig."

# Little Pig Is Back

## by Jane Simon
### illustrated by Pedro Vega

## Teacher/Family Member ................................................

### Character Discussion

Discuss the two characters in the story. What kind of character is Little Pig? How is the Big Pig different? Which character is more likeable?

 **School-Home Connection**

Invite your child to read aloud *Little Pig Is Back*. Help him or her read the dialogue in the story.

| | |
|---|---|
| Word Count: | 49 |
| Vocabulary Words: | back |
| | down |
| | get |
| | going |
| | little |
| | make |
| | said |
| | up |
| Phonic Elements: | Consonants: /n/ *n*, /k/ *ck*, *k* |
| | nap |
| | snack |

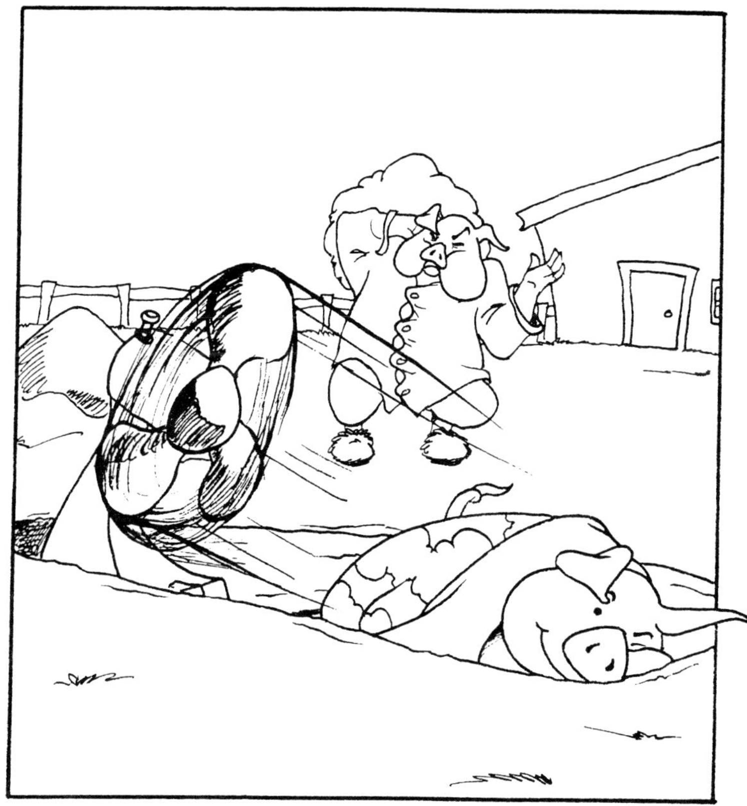

"Now I am going to nap," said Little Pig.

8

The pigs are in the house.

1

"Get up," said Little
Pig.

"I am going to get
a fan."

"Get back!" said
Little Pig.

6

"I am going to make
a snack."

"Get down," said
Little Pig.

"We are going back
here."

TAKE-HOME BOOK
**Together Again**
Use with "The Big, Big Wall."

Harcourt

# One, Two, Three, Kick!

by Catherine James
illustrated by Pedro Vega

## Teacher/Family Member....................................................

### Counting Help

With your child, think of tasks that require about three steps, such as brushing teeth, making a peanut butter sandwich, or planting a seed. Take turns describing each task using the words *one, two,* and *three* to explain.

### School-Home Connection

Invite your child to read aloud *One, Two, Three, Kick!* Help him or her understand the sequence in the story.

Word Count:            60

Vocabulary Words:      again
                       all
                       came
                       have
                       help
                       not
                       on
                       one
                       three
                       two
                       want

Phonic Elements:       Consonant: /l/; Phonogram: *-all*
                       all

I did it!
I did not have to
kick!

8

All of you, come and
help me!

1

One came to help.
Kick it again!

You will not get it in.
I am here now!

Harcourt

6

Two came to help.
Kick it again!

3

Three came to help.
Kick it again!

Come on!
Run and kick!

TAKE-HOME BOOK
*Join In*
Use with "What Day Is It?"

Harcourt

# Thank-You Day

## by Mary Louise Bourget
### illustrated by Pedro Vega

## Teacher/Family Member...............................................

### Thank You, Too

After children read the story, ask them to write a list of people they would like to thank for their help, kindness, or friendship.

### School-Home Connection

Invite your child to read *Thank-You Day* to you. Ask him or her what the boy in the story forgot to do.

Word Count: 60

Vocabulary Words:
day
forgot
happy
my
so
thank
they
this
was

Phonic Elements: Digraph: /th/*th*; Short vowel: /o/*o*
this
thank
Mom

Harcourt

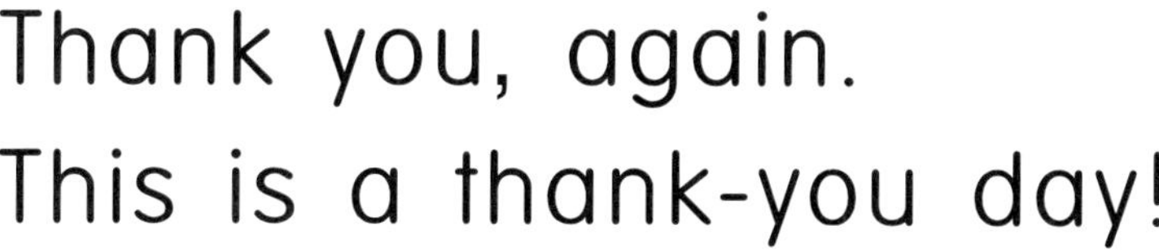

Thank you, again.
This is a thank-you day!

8

What a good day I had.

It was my day.
Mom and Dad had a
surprise.

I forgot to look in it!

Thank you, Mom!
Thank you, Dad!

6

They had a sack.
It was so big!

3

This makes me so happy!
This is what I wanted!

I forgot to thank you.

Harcourt

TAKE-HOME BOOK
*Join In*
Use with "Moving Day."

# Better Go

## by Robert Fletcher
### illustrated by Neil Posis

## Teacher/Family Member..............................................

### Safety Talk

Discuss home safety rules with children. Make a list showing where they should meet outside if there is a fire in the home, where they should go if they get lost in a store, etc.

 **School-Home Connection**

Invite your child to read *Better Go*. Help him or her find the question words *what* and *where* in the story. Together, make up new asking sentences using the words.

| | |
|---|---|
| Word Count: | 58 |
| Vocabulary Words: | better |
| | but |
| | go |
| | I'm |
| | like |
| | time |
| | were |
| | yes |
| Phonic Elements: | Consonant: /g/*g*; Double medial consonants |
| | digging |

Harcourt

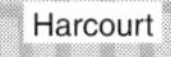

TIPTON ELEMENTARY PRIMARY

Here you are!
Where were you?

8

We are not happy.
We have to go.

1

I like the pond, but
I think I had better go.

2

What time is it now?
I want my snack!

7

Harcourt

What time is it?
Where is my hat?

6

I like digging, but
I think I had better go.

3

Now I'm going.

Yes, I'm going.

TAKE-HOME BOOK
*Join In*
Use with "How Many Fish?"

Harcourt

# So Many Fish!

**by Ryan Earl**
*illustrated by Darrin Johnston*

## Teacher/Family Member.................................................

### How Many In All?

Have children create addition stories by putting small objects, such as paper clips, into two groups of ten or less. They can ask a classmate questions about their groups, such as *How many paper clips in all?*

### School-Home Connection

Encourage your child to read aloud *So Many Fish!* After reading the last page, help your child count all the fish on the previous pages and then point to the correct answer.

Word Count:          94

Vocabulary Words:    fish
                     how
                     many
                     six
                     way

Phonic Elements:     Consonants: /r/ r, /f/ f, ff; /l/ ll, l
                     Fran
                     all
                     call

Fold

This way, that way,
Add them again, you see.
This way, that way,
add all the fish with me.

Are you good at math?
Here's a way to see.
Come and read now—
Can you add like me?

Fran has six fish.
Ming has four fish.

Now you make the call—
How many fish in all?

Harcourt

Three fish are happy.
Six fish are not.

Now you make the call—
How many fish in all?

Bill and Gill came in.
Todd and Ann came, too.

4

Now you make the call—
How many fish in all?

5

TAKE-HOME BOOK
*Join In*
Use with "Kit's Pajamas."

Harcourt

# The Best Home

by Leslie McHenry
illustrated by Jack Graham

## Teacher/Family Member ..........................................

### My Best Home

Talk with children about what makes a home feel comfortable and cozy.
Invite them to draw and color a picture of such a home.

### School-Home Connection

Invite your child to read aloud *The Best Home*. Help him or her read and
identify the action words in the story.

Word Count:            83

Vocabulary Words:      best
                       could
                       do
                       find
                       for
                       home
                       out
                       put
                       soon
                       their

Phonic Elements:       Consonant: /b/*b*; *R*-controlled vowel: /ôr/*or*
                       bag
                       forgot

Their home is the best!

We will make
the best home.

This could go here.
That could go out.
Put this on top.

2

I forgot one thing!
I will find it!

7

Harcourt

Do you like it?
Yes, it's the best!
Now I want a nap!

Find a bag for me.
Help me put this on.
Then we can mop.

Could you put this up?
Green looks better,
but I like pink.

Soon they had their
home. It looked so good.
What do you think?

TAKE-HOME BOOK
*Join In*
Use with "Where Do Frogs Come From?"

# Little Fish's Big Wish

## by Catherine James
### illustrated by Jack Graham

## Teacher/Family Member ..............................................

### Flash a Word

Ask your child to make a list of words that end with *-ish* and *-ash*. Use the list to make flash cards.

 **School-Home Connection**

Invite your child to read aloud *Little Fish's Big Wish*. Help him or her identify and read the dialogue in the story.

| | |
|---|---|
| Word Count: | 132 |
| Vocabulary Words: | does |
| | first |
| | from |
| | gone |
| | grow |
| | pushes |
| | eat |
| Phonic Elements: | Consonant: /w/*w*; Digraph: /sh/*sh* |
| | fish |
| | wish |
| | swam |
| | want |

Fold

"Thank you, Little Fish.
This does make a good
snack." Little Fish forgot
his wish and had his
snack.

8

A little fish swam in a
pond. He dashed in and
out of rocks.

1

He swam fast, but he was
not happy.
"I wish I were big," he
said. "I want to grow."

Little Fish was gone. First,
he got the rock with two
pushes. He picked the
plant.

"Little Fish, could you
pick that plant from there?
I'm too big to get it."

6

His mama swam in the
pond.
"Where has my little fish
gone?" she asked.

"I want to grow, Mama,"
said Little Fish. "The big
fish pushes me down."

4

"That's a big wish from a
little fish," said Mama
Fish. "First, does my little
fish want a snack to eat?"

5

Harcourt

TAKE-HOME BOOK
*Join In*
Use with "Daniel's Mystery Egg."

# Next Time

**by Lynn Downing**
*illustrated by Alex Delange*

## Teacher/Family Member................................................

### Waiting Time

Discuss things that keep children waiting. With your child, write on small strips of paper simple ideas to pass the time while waiting. Keep the strips handy for times when you wait in line, in traffic, or in a restaurant.

 **School-Home Connection**

Invite your child to read aloud *Next Time*. When the story is finished, talk about how the hen feels during the story.

Word Count: 117

Vocabulary Words:
ever
found
maybe
need
next
no
take
wait
white

Phonic Elements: Consonant: /ks/*x*; Short Vowel: /e/*e*
best
next
hen
egg
ten
get

Thank you, Hen! This
white egg is the best.
I'm so glad I found it.

How are you, Hen?
You do not have an
egg for me yet? Then I
will sit here and wait.

The next time I wait
for you, I'll take my
ball and bat.



You'll see. I don't need
to sit here for you,
Hen. No, I do not.

The next time I wait
for you, I'll take my
time and you'll need
to wait.

Maybe there will not
ever be a next time,
Hen.

The next time I wait
for you, maybe I'll be
ten.

If I ever get to ten, I
will not wait for you,
Hen. No, I will not.

Harcourt

TAKE-HOME BOOK
**Special Times**
Use with "Catch Me If You Can!"

# Tickle My Feet

## by Jane Simon
## illustrated by Alex Delange

## Teacher/Family Member ....................................................

### Who Am I?
Ask children to laugh like the duck in the story. Then ask a volunteer to laugh like another animal so everyone can guess which animal he or she is imitating. Have children take turns laughing like different animals.

 **School-Home Connection**

Invite your child to read aloud *Tickle My Feet*. Help him or her recognize who is speaking on each page.

| | |
|---|---|
| Word Count: | 110 |
| Vocabulary Words: | by |
| | feet |
| | hide |
| | much |
| | other |
| | when |
| | your |
| Phonic Elements: | Consonant Digraph: /ch/*tch, ch*; |
| | Consonant: /l/-*le* |
| | check |
| | tickle |
| | tickles |
| | itch |
| | itching |
| | scratch |

No! Do not hide! Do not
hide from me now! I beg
you—TICKLE MY FEET!

My feet itch. I need to
scratch them.

My feet are itching. Will you scratch my feet?



Does it tickle by your leg?
Does it tickle when I do this?
Maybe I need to stop.

That tickles! Yes, it does!
Now tickle the other one.
Ho! Ho! Ha! Ha! That
tickles so much!

Your feet are itching? When
did that happen? This isn't
good.

They itch so much. I beg you
to scratch them! Scratch this
one, then the other.

Let me see. I'll scratch your
feet by the legs and check
them, too.

TAKE-HOME BOOK
*Special Times*
Use with "When the TV Broke."

# Watch the Eggs

## by Nina Rivera
## illustrated by Len Epstein

## Teacher/Family Member

### Green Egg Game

Cut out egg shapes from green construction paper. Write each Vocabulary Word (see below) on two different eggs. Have children turn the eggs over and mix them up. Direct them to take turns turning over two eggs at a time and reading the words to find a match.

### School-Home Connection

Invite your child to read aloud *Watch the Eggs*. Then take turns reading the parts of the brother and sister.

| | |
|---|---|
| Word Count: | 147 |
| Vocabulary Words: | every |
| | made |
| | nothing |
| | right |
| | sister |
| | some |
| | turned |
| | watched |
| | week |
| Phonic Elements: | Consonant: /y/*y*; *R*-Controlled Vowel: /är/*ar* |
| | yes |
| | yelled |
| | smart |

"It's simple," I said.
"When eggs sit, they turn
green. Don't wait to eat
your eggs. See you next
week."

One day my sister made
some eggs. This is what
happened.

"Every time I make this,
it's not right," my sister
yelled. "Nothing is right!"

2

"Do they turn green every
time?" I asked. "Did this
happen last week?"
"Yes. That's right," she
said.

7

Harcourt

"You made a call," I said.
"Yes, and when I came
back, the eggs had turned
green!" she said.

"What did you make?" I
asked. My sister thinks
she's smart, but she needs
my help.

"Yes," I said. "Then what happened?"

"Nothing. I turned off the gas," she said. "I made a call. I left the eggs in the pan."

"I made some eggs. I put some eggs in the pan. I turned on the gas. I watched the eggs as they got hot."

TAKE-HOME BOOK
*Special Times*
Use with "Too Much Talk!"

# Why Don't You Go Away?

by Sarah Holiday
*illustrated by Alex Delange*

## Teacher/Family Member.................................................

### Animal Friends

Have children make a list of animals who might live in the tree with the baby bird. Talk about what these animals eat and where they live in the tree.

 **School-Home Connection**

Invite your child to read aloud *Why Don't You Go Away?* Help him or her identify all the animals in the story.

Word Count:          136

Vocabulary Words:      about
                       always
                       away
                       don't
                       who
                       why

Phonic Elements: Consonants: /j/*j*; /z/*z, zz*; /kw/*qu*;
                 Short Vowel: /u/*u*
                 jumping
                 quick
                 buzz
                 bug
                 running
                 run
                 zap
                 but

MAMA! It's you! It's about time! Do you have something for me to eat?

8

I am waiting for my mama. She will bring me a snack.

1

Who is jumping on my nest?
Is it Mama? I always like it
when she has something
to eat.



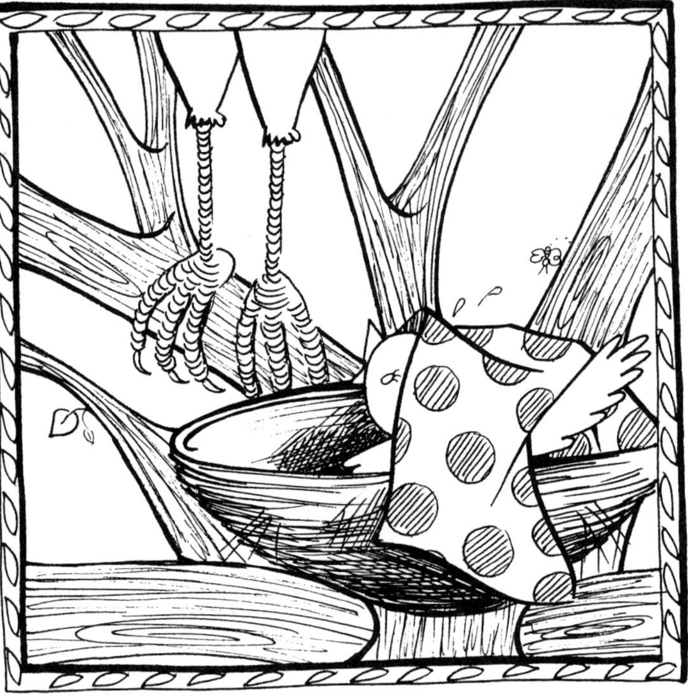

I see two feet on my nest.
They are so big! I want to
run, but I can't. Why don't
you go away?

Who is there? Is it you,
Mama?
Is anyone there? Can anyone
help me? My mama forgot
about me.

It's not my mama! Why
don't you go? Quick! Run
away now.

Who is running to my nest?
Mama, is that you? I always
like a snack from Mama.

It's a big bug! You are not my
mama! Why don't you go?
Buzz off! My mama will
zap you!

Harcourt

TAKE-HOME BOOK
*Special Times*
Use with "Making Friends, Keeping Friends."

Fold

# "More!" Says Our Evan

## by Kristina Mario
### illustrated by Christian Slade

## Teacher/Family Member..........................................

### Adding Game

Use the story to practice addition facts using the number 1. Start with
1 + 1 = 2  2 + 1 = 3, and continue to 10. If children need help with the
concept, use counters or pennies.

### School-Home Connection

Invite your child to read aloud *"More!" Says Our Evan*. Together, review
the addition in the story.

| | |
|---|---|
| Word Count: | 95 |

| | |
|---|---|
| Vocabulary Words: | each |
| | more |
| | our |
| | over |
| | plays |
| | says |
| | there |
| | these |

| | |
|---|---|
| Phonic Elements: | Consonant: /v/ *v* |
| | Evan |
| | seven |

Harcourt

TIPTON ELEMENTARY PRIMARY

Each day I add, one by
one.
Playing over and over—
it's so much fun!

8

Every day, Evan and I
play. He is the best,
always.

1

Evan wants to do each
thing I do.
If he has one, he wants
one more.
"More!" says our Evan.

Now there are seven.

No one plays blocks as
much as Evan.
He has six and wants one
more.
"More!" says our Evan.

6

Now there are two.

3

"There you are. Take these
from me."
He has two and wants
one more.
"More!" says our Evan.

Now there are three.

4

5

TAKE-HOME BOOK
**Special Times**
Use with "Digger Pig and the Turnip."

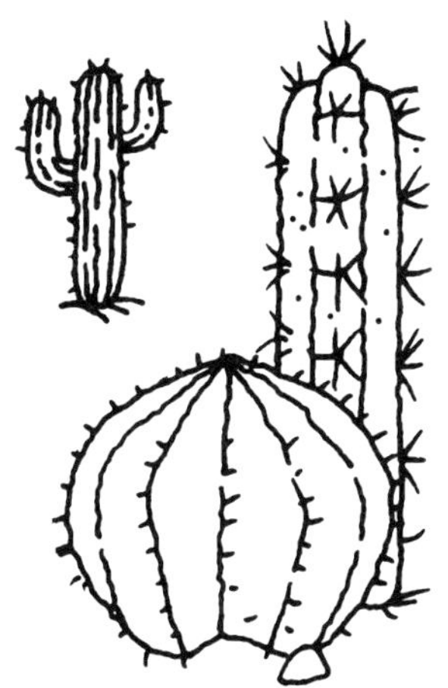

# In the Desert

## by Lynn Downing
## illustrated by Ken Bowser

## Teacher/Family Member.................................................

### Desert Facts

With children, make a list of desert facts—things that children know about the desert. Then invite them to draw pictures of the desert.

 **School-Home Connection**

Invite your child to read aloud *In the Desert*. Talk about desert animals and how they survive in a dry, hot place.

Word Count: 151

Vocabulary Words:
around
myself
used

Phonic Elements: *R*-Controlled Vowels: /ûr/*ur, er, ir*
desert
burning
birds
runners
different
curl
other

Maybe you'll see me—a
jackrabbit. I am fast! I
hop past other animals.
I hop past jackrabbits
like myself, too!

If you go to the desert,
look around. The desert is
full of animals and plants.
You can see many
different living things.

The desert is a garden,
but it is hot. Plants that
grow here are used for
many things.

Sometimes there is a
small pond in the desert.
There you could see a
desert pupfish. It is a
very small fish.

There are birds in the
desert. They like plants
and shrubs where bugs
buzz around.

6

The land in a desert may
be flat. It could be full of
rocks and sand.

3

The kit fox is at home in
the desert. This small fox
is a very good hunter.

4

Lizards are good runners.
They like to curl up in the
burning sun, too. They use
rocks for hiding.

5

TAKE-HOME BOOK
**Special Times**
Use with "Rex and Lilly Playtime."

Harcourt

# Ready, Set, Dance!

**by Maria Velasquez**
*Illustrated by Len Epstein*

## Teacher/Family Member................................................

### Make a Dance

Have children work independently or in small groups to make up a simple dance that they can teach others.

### School-Home Connection

Invite your child to read aloud *Ready, Set, Dance!* Reinforce the rhyming words by clapping rhythmically as you reread the story together.

Word Count:          112

Vocabulary Words:    dance
                     how
                     music
                     ready
                     shall
                     teacher

Phonic Elements:     Long Vowel: /o/*oa, ow*
                     show

Harcourt

Teacher, teacher, I'm ready
for the show.
Teacher, teacher, come on!
Let's go!

One, two, three—
Get ready, get set, DANCE!

Teacher, teacher, tell us
how to dance!
Teacher, teacher, play the
music fast!



Are you going to dance?
Are you going to sing?
How about some music?
Grab the bells and ring!

Harcourt

Teacher, teacher, shall we tap?
Teacher, teacher, shall we snap?

6

Are you ready to dance?
Are you ready to sing?
How about some music?
Now you do your thing!

3

Teacher, teacher, play
some more!
Teacher, teacher, I'll play
my horn!

Are you set to dance?
Are you set to sing?
How about some music?
Turn your partner and
swing!

TAKE-HOME BOOK
**Welcome Home**
Use with "A Bed Full of Cats."

# A Day with Wiggles

by Dana Catharine
*illustrated by Toni Goffe*

## Teacher/Family Member ·············································

**Cat Poem**

Write the letters in the name *Wiggles* down the left side of a piece of paper. Have children write a word that begins with each letter to describe the cat.

 **School-Home Connection**

Listen as your child reads *A Day with Wiggles* to you. Ask what your child thinks was the best thing Wiggles and the boy did.

| | |
|---|---|
| Word Count: | 209 |

Vocabulary Words:
room
write
try
please
hear
moved
should
only
full

Phonic Elements:  Long Vowel: /ē/*e, ee, ea*

| | | |
|---|---|---|
| she | sleeps | |
| me | feed | eat |
| tree | treat | we |

Harcourt

This time, I can because
Wiggles is tired. She has gone to
sleep on my bed.

**12**

Wiggles is my cat. What do
you think she does all day?
Most of the day, she sleeps in
my room!

**1**

Wiggles follows me everywhere
I go. I like to write. I try to
write about Wiggles.

**2**

I go to my room and take out
my book. I want to write about
what Wiggles did today.

**11**

Harcourt

I am hungry now, so I go in.
Wiggles follows me. I get a treat
for myself. Wiggles gets a cat
treat.

Wiggles sits on the book I am
trying to write in today.

"Please, Wiggles," I say. "Will you get off my book?"

Wiggles doesn't hear me, so I move her. That cat! She moves right back!

4

She tries to get the bugs, but the bugs are too quick!

9

Harcourt

The grass is full of bugs. The
bugs hop. Wiggles hops, too.

**8**

Every morning, I feed
Wiggles. Then I feed myself.
Wiggles will eat only when
I do.

**5**

I go out. Wiggles does, too. I go up into the big tree. Wiggles thinks about what she should do.

She tries to come up with me. Then we go down. Wiggles takes a big jump. She flies down!

6

7

Harcourt

TAKE-HOME BOOK
**Welcome Home**
Use with "Me on the Map."

# Our Town

**by Julie Verne**
***illustrated by Anne Kennedy***

## Teacher/Family Member

### On a Map

Have your child draw a make-believe map of Sam's town, showing the places where his friends work.

 **School-Home Connection**

Invite your child to read *Our Town* to you. Then talk about people your child sees in your town and the jobs they have.

| | |
|---|---|
| Word Count: | 237 |

| | |
|---|---|
| Vocabulary Words: | Earth |
| | world |
| | United States of America |
| | country |
| | town |
| | place |
| | special |

| | |
|---|---|
| Phonic Elements: | Long Vowel: /ā/a-e |
| | name |
| | Kate |
| | Jake |
| | bakes |
| | cakes |
| | Gabe |

Now tell me about your town. Where on this Earth do you live? Who are your friends? What special jobs do they have?

**12**

Hello, I'm Sam. I live in a part of the world called the United States of America. That is the name of my country.

**1**

Come see my town. It is a
special place. You can meet
some of my friends.



I showed you my town.
You met some of my friends.
You found out about their
special jobs.

"Hello, Mrs. Smith."

Mrs. Smith is my friend.
She has a special job here in
town. She is a teacher.

10

"Hello, Jim. Hello, Kate."
Jim and Kate are my
friends. They have a special
job here in town. They help
people.

3

"Hello, Jake."
Jake is my friend. He has a special job here in town. He keeps our town safe.

4

"Hello, Dr. Fong."
Dr. Fong is my friend. He has a special job here in town. He helps sick animals.

9

"Hello, Gabe."

Gabe is my friend. She has
a special job here in town.
She fixes the roads.

8

"Hello, Pam."

Pam is my friend. She has
a special job here in town.
She brings letters to people.

5

"Hello, Pepe."
Pepe is my friend. Pepe
has a special job that I like!
He bakes cakes and cookies.

6

"Hello, Bess."
Bess is my friend. She has
a special job here in town.
She picks up cans and glass.

7

Harcourt

TAKE-HOME BOOK
**Welcome Home**
Use with "Lilly's Busy Day."

**by Fernando Ruiz**
*illustrated by Marion Eldridge*

## Teacher/Family Member .......................................

### Hide-and-Seek

Ask your child to tell where Little Rabbit was hiding in the story. Then look in nature books and magazines to find out where real rabbits hide.

 **School-Home Connection**

Invite your child to read *Sister Rabbit* to you. Then ask your child to tell whether he or she liked the story and to explain why or why not.

Word Count: 193

Vocabulary Words:
most
nice
before
laugh
thought
carry

Phonic Elements:
Long Vowel: /ē/*y, ie*
easy
funny
everywhere
bunny

"There you are!" said
Big Sister. "You funny little
bunny! Now I will carry you
inside. You can run to your
bed for a nap!"

**12**

Big Sister is a rabbit-sitter.
Does that mean she sits on
little rabbits? No, she doesn't
sit on little rabbits.

**1**

She sits *for* little rabbits
the way a baby-sitter sits for
you. That's why she is a
called rabbit-sitter!

Big Sister still could not
find Little Rabbit. Then Little
Rabbit popped out!

Harcourt

Big Sister looked just
about everywhere!

Most of the time, rabbit-
sitting is easy and fun. When
Mama Rabbit goes out, she
asks Big Sister to watch
Little Rabbit.

Big Sister reads to Little Rabbit. She makes Little Rabbit's lunch and plays games with Little Rabbit.

**4**

Big Sister looked there.

**9**

Big Sister looked here.

Then Big Sister takes Little Rabbit outside. That is nice for Little Rabbit and Big Sister, too.

One day, Big Sister was playing with Little Rabbit in the yard. They had played tag there before.

6

Big Sister started to laugh. She thought Little Rabbit was funny. Then, Big Sister did not laugh. She couldn't find Little Rabbit!

7

TAKE-HOME BOOK
***Welcome Home***
Use with "Splash!"

Answers: Sentences 1, 3, 4, and 6 are true.

# All About Bears

**by Betsy Franco**
***illustrated by Rosiland Solomon***

## Teacher/Family Member ..............................................

### Follow That Bear!

Have your child read the sentences and decide which ones tell something true about grizzly bears. Together, write one more fact about bears. (Turn the page to find the answers.)

1. Bears eat ripe fruits, grass, meat, and bark.
2. Bears cannot stand on two legs.
3. Baby bears are born in a den.
4. A bear can be 8 feet tall.
5  Bears do not like to eat fish.
6. In winter a bear lives on fat from its body.

 **School-Home Connection**

Listen as your child reads *All About Bears* to you. Then have your child tell some things he or she learned about grizzly bears.

| Word Count: | 229 | | |
|---|---|---|---|
| | | | |
| Vocabulary Words: | bears | sound | sorry |
| | while | once | together |
| | | | |
| Phonic Elements: | Long Vowel: /ī/i-e | | |
| | like | wise | time | sometimes |
| | outside | size | hide | dive |
| | inside | ripe | | |

Harcourt

Once my cubs can see well,
we can go outside together.
When they are bigger, they
will leave me. They will go
off to live on their own!

Look at me. What kind of
bear am I?

I am a grizzly bear. You can
tell by the bump on my back.
Grizzly bears like me live in
North America.

2

These are my baby bears.
They are about the size of
a mouse. When will they go
outside?

11

In winter, I will go to sleep
inside a den. While I sleep,
I will live on fat from my
body. My cubs will be born
in the den.

10

Look at me when I stand on
my back legs. How tall do
you think I am?

3

I am 8 feet tall! I am
standing up because I hear
a sound. I am looking
for danger.

4

It will be winter soon. What
will I do? Where will I go?

9

Grizzly bears eat ripe fruits, grass, meat, and bark. We like to dive after fish. I am always sorry if I do not catch a big one.

Sometimes I see people hiking together. What do I do?

Most of the time, I run and
hide. Sometimes bears will
not run away. Never go up
to a bear. That would not be
wise. Bears are wild.

I am hungry. What do I like
to eat?

TAKE-HOME BOOK
*Welcome Home*
Use with "My Robot."

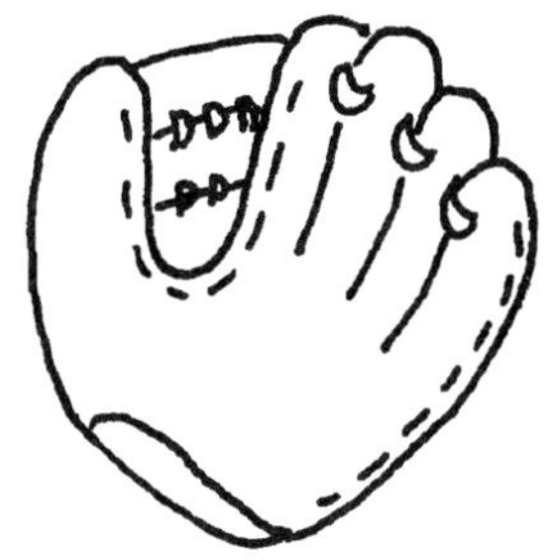

# Can We Play Now?

**by David Webb**
**illustrated by Laurel Aiello**

## Teacher/Family Member ...............................................

### Where Did They Go?

Have your child draw pictures to show three places where Kim and Ling looked for the baseball equipment. He or she should then write *1, 2,* and *3* to show where the girls went first, second, and third.

 **School-Home Connection**

Invite your child to read *Can We Play Now?* to you. Ask why Kim thought that Ling was the best friend of all.

Word Count:         239

Vocabulary Words:

heard
pretty
children
new
school
almost

Phonic Elements:

Consonant: /s/*c*

place     nice
raced    space

Digraph: /hw/*wh*

when
while    white

"Almost," Kim said with a smile. "First I need to say something. Thank you for helping me. Thank you for being the best friend of all!"

**12**

Kim heard the doorbell ring. "Let's play ball," said Ling.

"OK," said Kim. "I need to look for my ball."

"I will help you," said Ling.

**1**

Kim and Ling looked all over the place. Kim's room was pretty messy.

The children picked things up. Soon there was much more space in the shed.

"Here is my bat," said Kim.

"Can we play *now*?" asked Ling.

The children raced to the
white shed. They looked all
over the place. The shed was
pretty messy.

**10**

The children picked things
up. They put things away.
Soon Kim's room was nice
and clean.

**3**

"Here is my ball," shouted
Kim. "Isn't it nice? It's new."
"It *is* nice," said Ling.
"Can we play now? Let's
play at the school."

**4**

"When I find my bat, we
can go," said Kim.
"I will help you look,"
said Ling.

**9**

"Here is my mitt," shouted
Kim. "It is a nice, new mitt."

"Can we play now?" asked
Ling. "Let's go to the school."

"Where is my mitt?" said
Kim.

"I will help you look,"
said Ling.

The children went to the
playroom. They looked all
over the place. The playroom
was pretty messy.

**6**

The children picked things
up while they looked. They
put things away. Soon the
playroom was spic and span.

**7**

Harcourt

TAKE-HOME BOOK
***Welcome Home***
Use with "The Absent-Minded Toad."

# Joey Goes to Market

**by Dottie Makem**
***illustrated by Dave Sullivan***

Harcourt

## Teacher/Family Member ........................................

**Draw This!**
Have your child draw pictures of things Joey got at the market and tell what Joey and his dad will make with each one.

 **School-Home Connection**
Invite your child to read *Joey Goes to Market* to you. Then ask what your child would buy at the market to make vegetable soup.

Word Count:        253

Vocabulary Words:        blue
                         warm
                         smiled
                         buy
                         colors
                         orange

Phonic Elements:        Vowel variant: /ou/*ow*
                        town
                        down
                        wow
                        now
                        how

"We have many pretty colors
now!" said Joey.

"Yes," said Dad, "but how
can we make vegetable soup?
We don't have any vegetables!"

**12**

"Wake up!" said Joey's dad.
"It's Saturday. The sky is blue,
and it's warm outside. Let's go
to the market in town."

**1**

Joey jumped out of bed and ran down to eat. He smiled thinking about going to the market with his dad.

Dad smiled. "Yes, we can buy some grapes," he said. "We don't need grapes for vegetable soup, but we can make some jam with them."

"How about these red grapes, Dad?" asked Joey. "Can we buy them? I like the color red. Let's put them in the soup!"

**10**

"We can buy vegetables at the market," Dad said to Joey. "Then we can make vegetable soup."

**3**

"Look at the vegetables!" said
Dad. "We can make good soup."

"Wow! Look at all the colors!"
Joey said. "I like vegetables with
pretty colors!"

**4**

Dad laughed. "Yes, we can
buy some apples," he said.
"We don't need apples for
vegetable soup, but we can
bake a pie with them."

**9**

Harcourt

"How about these green
apples, Dad?" asked Joey.
"Can we buy them? I like the
color green. Let's put them
in the soup!"

**8**

"Look at these big oranges.
Can we buy some now?" asked
Joey. "I like the color orange.
Let's put them in the soup!"

**5**

"Yes, we can buy some
oranges," answered Dad.

"We don't need oranges for
vegetable soup," he said. "But
let's buy some and make an
orange drink."

Harcourt

TAKE-HOME BOOK
**Welcome Home**
Use with "Tumbleweed Stew."

by James McGuire
*illustrated by Dave Blanchette*

## Teacher/Family Member .........................................

### Counting Rhymes
Share familiar counting rhymes with your child, such as "One, Two, Buckle My Shoe" and "1, 2, 3, 4, 5, I Caught a Fish Alive."

 ### School-Home Connection
Ask your child to read *The Little Animals' Big Feast* to you. Then ask your child to think of other animals that could come to the feast. Have your child make up more pages for the story.

| Word Count: | 198 |
|---|---|
| Vocabulary Words: | might |
| | fire |
| | cook |
| | food |
| | great |
| | water |
| | heads |
| | took |

Phonic Elements: Long Vowel: /ī/*y, ie*

| pie | my |
|---|---|
| fry | try |
| fly | why |
| sky | good-by |

One little skunk
Sat on his trunk.
"Good-by! Good-by!"
he said. "Oh, my!"

**12**

One little skunk
sat on a trunk.
"I might make some pie!"
he said. "Oh, my!"

**1**

Two little cats
sat on their mats.
"These potatoes we'll fry!"
they said. "Oh, my!"

**2**

Two little cats
Took out their nice mats.
"You will soon see why!"
they said. "Good-by!"

**11**

Harcourt

Three little dogs
Jumped onto their logs.
"Oh, look at the sky!"
they said. "Good-by!"

**10**

Three little dogs
sat on some logs.
"A cake we will try,"
they said. "Oh, my!"

**3**

Four little chicks
sat on some sticks.
"For hot dogs we might fly!"
they said. "Oh, my!"

**4**

Four little chicks
rested their heads on sticks.
"It's late. We should fly!"
they said. "Good-by!"

**9**

Five little ducks
got into their trucks.
"Let's make water fly,"
they said. "Good-by!"

Five little ducks
sat in their trucks.
"Some fruit we will buy,"
they said. "Oh, my!"

A fire was lit
to cook in the pit.
The hot food was great!
Skunk cleaned his plate.

**6**

Five, four, three, two, one,
Skunk's pals had some fun.
"Your pie is the best,"
They all said, "Oh my!"

**7**

Harcourt

TAKE-HOME BOOK
**Welcome Home**
Use with "Little Bear's Friend."

**by Jeannie Graham**
*illustrated by Ruth Flanigan*

Harcourt

## Teacher/Family Member .............................................

### Sing a Song of Friends

With your child, sing songs about making friends, such as "Make New Friends, but Keep the Old" and "The More We Get Together."

 **School-Home Connection**

Ask your child to read *Over the Gate* to you. Then ask your child to tell five things he or she would do with a new friend.

| | |
|---|---|
| Word Count: | 226 |
| Vocabulary Words: | love |
| | climb |
| | began |
| | name |
| Phonic Elements: | Long Vowel: /ō/*o-e* |
| | home |
| | hope |
| | rope |
| | rode |
| | hole |
| | alone |
| | stones |
| | cones |
| | jokes |

Now Marco plays with Lucy and Don every day. They jump rope. They tell jokes and laugh. Marco loves his new home now.

Moving is hard! When Marco moved, he missed his old home very much.

"I miss our old house," Marco
said to Mom. "I miss my
friends," Marco said to Dad.

2

"Hello. My name is Marco.
I just moved here."

"We just moved here, too,"
the girl said. "My name is Lucy.
This is Don."

11

Marco began to climb. When he got to the top, he peeked over the gate.



"We know," Mom and Dad said. "We miss our old home, too, but you will make new friends. We hope you will love this home one day."

Every day, Marco played
outside. He jumped rope. He
rode his bike. He picked up
stones. Marco had fun, but he
was alone.

"I know!" thought Marco. "I
will climb up on this. Then I
can look over."

Marco looked through a hole.
He couldn't see anyone and he
couldn't open the gate. "How
can I find out who is over
there?" he wondered.

8

Marco played with his Mom
and Dad. They played ball and
got ice cream cones, but Marco
did not meet any friends.

5

Then one day Marco heard
something. It was something he
had not heard in a long time.

HE HEARD CHILDREN
PLAYING!

6

7

TAKE-HOME BOOK
*Set Sail*
Use with "The Story of a Blue Bird."

**by Dana Catharine**
*illustrated by Bill Ogden*

## Teacher/Family Member ...........................................

### I Think I Can!

Ask children to share things that were difficult for them to learn. Encourage them to tell how they felt when they tried the activity for the first time.

 **School-Home Connection**

Invite your child to read *Fly Away!* to you. Ask your child how the girl helped the birds. Then ask how the birds helped the girl.

Word Count: 306

Vocabulary Words:
flew
learn
afraid
joined

Phonic Elements:
Long Vowel: /ī/*igh*

| | |
|---|---|
| high | bright |
| right | might |
| flight | tight |
| sunlight | night |

Inflections: *-ed, -ing* (drop final e)

| | |
|---|---|
| making | using |
| moved | loved |
| riding | |

"Will you help me learn to ride my bike?" I asked my mom and dad. Then, just like the baby birds, I tried and tried. Now, look at me. I'm riding!

**12**

I put up a bird feeder outside my room. I like to feed the birds. They eat the seeds I put out. They sing to me.

**1**

Last spring, two birds flew right up to my feeder. They began making a little nest.

I have a bright red bike.
At first, I wouldn't ride it.
I was afraid I might fall. Then I thought about the baby birds.
They were not afraid to fly.

Soon all three little birds were flying high in the bright sunlight. They loved flying!

I watched the birds every day. I wanted to learn how they made their nest. They were using sticks, dirt, and leaves.

Harcourt

One day, I saw three eggs in the nest. The mama bird sat on the eggs. She sat there day after day. Sometimes she moved the eggs around a little.

All day, the baby birds tried to fly. The mama and papa birds watched. That night, the baby birds flew into the roses.

4

9

The nest was so high! The
other two babies were afraid
they'd fall but they tried to fly.
Soon, they flew down to the
grass. They joined the other
baby bird.

**8**

Then one day, I saw three
baby birds in the nest! They
were very small. I could hear
them chirping. I thought that
they might want some food.

**5**

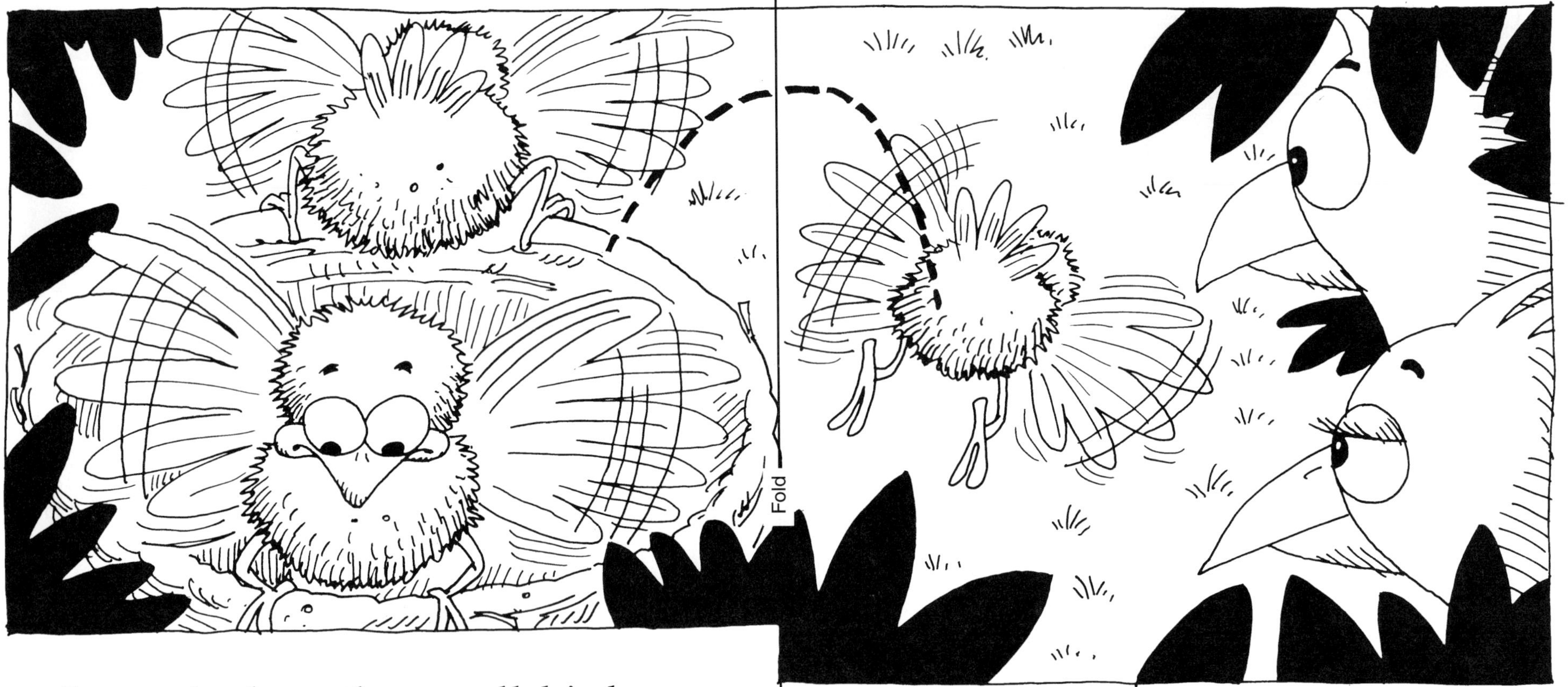

I watched as the small birds grew and grew. They sat on the side of the nest and looked out. They held on tight and flapped their wings.

**6**

Soon it was time for the baby birds to learn to fly. One baby bird flew out of the nest. It was a short flight!

**7**

TAKE-HOME BOOK
*Set Sail*
Use with "Frog and Toad All Year."

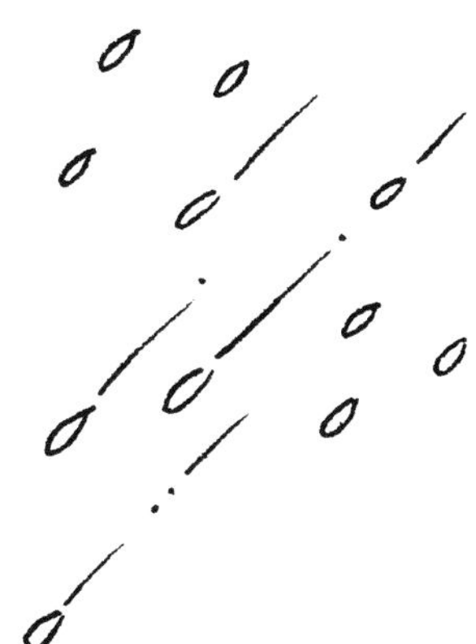

# Change of Plans

**by David Webb**
*illustrated by Anne Kennedy*

## Teacher/Family Member ·············································

### Raindrops

Gather a box top and a centimeter ruler. Then go outside with your child on a rainy day and catch raindrops on the box top. When you go inside, have your child measure the raindrops. How big was the biggest raindrop? the smallest?

 **School-Home Connection**

Ask your child to read *Change of Plans* to you. Together, make up sound effects for the raindrops and add them when rereading.

| | |
|---|---|
| Word Count: | 276 |

| | |
|---|---|
| Vocabulary Words: | son |
| | caught |
| | near |
| | cold |
| | sure |
| | working |

| | | |
|---|---|---|
| Phonic Elements: | Long Vowel: /ā/ *ai, ay* | |
| | rain | day |
| | raindrops | way |
| | raincoats | play |
| | | stay |

I was working hard.

"Now look outside," said Dad.
"The sun is shining again!"

"That's great!" I said.
"Changing plans is fun!"

12

I am Pablo and this is my dad. I will tell you about the day that Dad and I just had. We had a change of plans!

1

We were walking to the pool when it started to rain. The rain came down very hard. We were caught in it without our raincoats.

**2**

"Look, Dad!" I said. "The raindrops are not the same size. Some drops are as small as a pinhole. Other drops are as big as a quarter!"

**11**

I caught some raindrops.
"Now what?" I asked.
"We will find the size of each
drop," said Dad.

**10**

"It's OK, Son," said Dad. "We
are near home. Let's run!" So
we ran all the way home!

**3**

We were soaking wet and pretty cold, so we put on some dry clothes.

"We can't go to the pool now," I said. "What will we do?"

"Take this part of the box outside, Son" Dad said. "Let rain drop on it. Make sure you don't stay out too long. It should not get too wet."

"We will use one side of this box," said Dad. "Let's cut it up."

We cut the box. Then I said, "How will this catch rain?"

"We will have to change our plans," said Dad. "Sometimes it's fun to do something new."

8

5

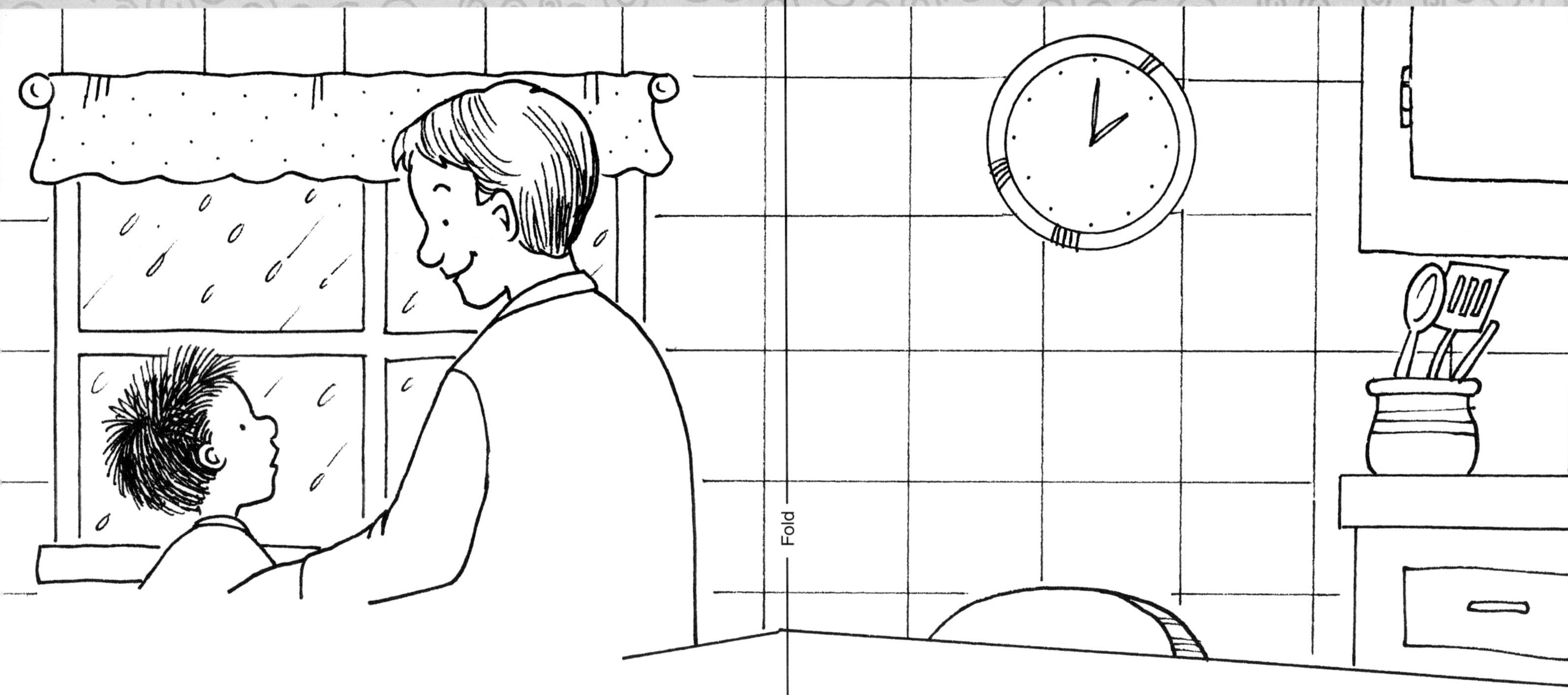

I wanted to play outside.
Then Dad said, "Let's do
something with rain."
"What will we do?"
I wondered.

"You can catch some
raindrops," said Dad. "We can
find out how big they are."
I wondered how we could
catch raindrops.

TAKE-HOME BOOK
*Set Sail*
Use with "The Puddle."

# I Go Out in the Rain to Play

**by Betsy Franco**
**illustrated by Jackie Snider**

## Teacher/Family Member

**Make Rain**

Boil a pot of water. Have your child put ice cubes in a pie pan. Use an oven mitt to hold the pan over the rising steam. Watch as drops of "rain" fall from the bottom of the pan. Ask your child how the mixture of hot air and cool air makes rain.

 **School-Home Connection**

Invite your child to read *I Go Out in the Rain to Play* to you. Then ask your child to find the rhyming words in each verse and to use them in rhyming sentences about rainy days.

| | | | |
|---|---|---|---|
| Word Count: | 174 | | |
| Vocabulary: | listen | told | largest |
| | course | different | care |
| Phonic Elements: | Long vowel: /ī/*i:* | | |
| | find | giant | |
| | mind | kind | |

Fold

Sun, sun,
Go away!
I love to go out
In the rain to play!

**12**

I listen to the
Dripping drops.
I run outside.
The drops don't stop.

**1**

The rain falls down
From way up high.
I run outside.
Mom gives a sigh.

2

Oh, no! I see
A yellow light.
Could it be stopping?
Yes, it might!

11

I do not care.
I do not mind
A drip-drop day
Of just this kind!

My dad told me
The other night
The sky is crying.
Is that right?

I will find
The largest drop.
Will it make
A giant plop?

My friend goes home.
She takes her boat.
My dog gets mud
All over my coat!

We float the boat,
And watch it go.
My dog sees it.
Of course–Oh, no!

8

Watch me run
Down the hill.
Oh, no! I'm slipping!
Now I'm still.

5

I'll find a different
Game to play.
I'll stay out in
The rain all day!

Here comes my friend.
She has her boat.
She says, "Let's see
If it will float."

Harcourt

TAKE-HOME BOOK
*Set Sail*
Use with "Poppleton Everyday."

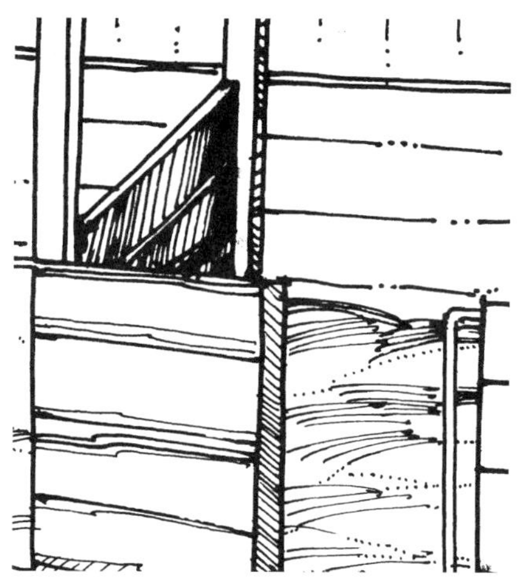

Answers:  1. horse;   2. hen;   3. cow;   4. pig;   5. Mike and Jane

**by Fernando Ruiz**
*illustrated by Len Ebert*

## Teacher/Family Member ...........................................

**Where Am I?**

Provide paper, and have your child draw a picture to show who in the story is saying each sentence. (Turn the page to find the answers.)

1. I sometimes sleep standing up in my farmyard bed.
2. My farmyard bed is sometimes in a tree.
3. Sometimes my farmyard bed is the grass.
4. My farmyard bed can be in the mud.
5. Our farmyard beds are in a tent.

 **School-Home Connection**

Ask your child to read *Farmyard Beds* to you. Then ask which farmyard bed your child thinks is the best.

| | | | |
|---|---|---|---|
| Word Count: | 269 | | |
| | | | |
| Vocabulary Words: | air | few | both |
| | edge | boy | brought |
| | | | |
| Phonic Elements: | Long Vowel: /ō/*o* | | |
| | going | hello | cold |
| | go | both | most |

"These beds are for a girl and a boy and a grampa," says Grampa. "I brought everything we need to have our own farmyard beds!"

Mike and Jane are looking at beds today, but they're not going to the bed shop! Where are they going?

They are going to Grampa's
farm. "Hello, Mike and Jane,"
says Grampa. "Let's look at
some of the beds on my farm."

"There is one more kind of
farmyard bed," says Grampa.
"Who is it for?" asks Mike.
"Come and see," Grampa says.

Harcourt

"Most of my hens sleep in the henhouse," says Grampa. "Look up in that tree. One of my hens made a bed up there!"

"I see some pigs," says Jane. "Where do pigs sleep at night? Do they sleep out here in the fresh air?"

"A few pigs make beds in the mud," Grampa says. "But most pigs don't like the cold air. They go inside to sleep in beds of hay."

**4**

"Where do the hens sleep, Grampa?" asks Jane. "Do they sleep out in the fresh air?"

**9**

"Some cows sleep outside,"
Grampa goes on. "The grass is
their bed, but some of them
sleep in the barn. Their babies
sleep in beds of hay."

**8**

"I see sheep and goats and
horses and cows," says Mike.
"Do they all sleep out here in
the fresh air?"

**5**

"Both the sheep and the goats
have beds inside," says Grampa.
"But they sleep in the hay at the
edge of the shed, too."

**6**

"These stalls are beds for the
horses," says Grampa. "Did you
know that horses can sleep
standing up in their beds?"

**7**

Harcourt

TAKE-HOME BOOK
*Set Sail*
Use with "Moon Rope."

# John Glenn in Space Again

by Isabella Cummings
illustrated by Dave Sullivan

## Teacher/Family Member ·············································

### Spaceships

Set out cardboard tubes, foil, and other art scraps. Invite children to create replicas of both spaceships in which John Glenn traveled into space.

 **School-Home Connection**

Ask your child to read *John Glenn in Space Again* to you. Ask how he or she feels about John Glenn.

| | |
|---|---|
| Word Count: | 269 |
| Vocabulary Words: | break |
| | idea |
| | quietly |
| | clear |
| | appear |
| Phonic Elements: | Long Vowel: /(y) $\overline{oo}$/u-e |
| | use |
| | capsule |
| | Consonant: /j/g, *dge* |
| | age |

·····················································

When I was writing a space story, I had an idea. I took a break and watched a program about John Glenn. I listened quietly and got to know a lot about a brave man.

What a great space story! Now that I know about this brave man, I can write a better story about him.

John Glenn has traveled into space two times. The first time, he went up in a space capsule that was attached to a rocket. The capsule was called *Friendship 7.*



# Landing

Many people waited for *Discovery* to return to Earth. When it landed, crowds appeared happy for John Glenn and his shuttle mates. People wondered how John Glenn, the oldest man in space, would feel.

Harcourt

John Glenn and his six shuttle
mates flew in space for nine
days. This was much longer
than that first flight he took
long ago.

**10**

John Glenn was the first
American to go around the
Earth. He flew around the Earth
three times in the space capsule.

**3**

# Friendship 7

*Friendship 7* was very small, but John Glenn was very brave. He brought it back to Earth safely.

4

# Lift-Off

*Discovery* was attached to a rocket. On a clear day in October 1998, *Discovery* went up. John Glenn was in space again!

9

He flew on the shuttle called
*Discovery* with six other people.

8

In 1998, John Glenn's age
was 77. At that time, he was
the oldest person to travel
into space.

5

If he was scared, he didn't let
it show. He appeared excited
and happy.

**6**

# 1998

This time he flew in a space
shuttle, not a space capsule.

**7**

Harcourt

TAKE-HOME BOOK
**Set Sail**
Use with "The Big Big Sea."

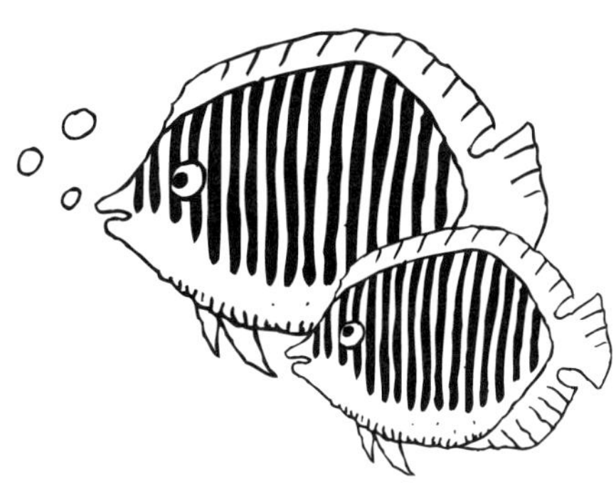

Answers:  1. sea horse;   2. long-nosed butterfly fish

# by James McGuire
# illustrated by Bill Ogden

## Teacher/Family Member ·····································

### That's Fishy!
Read the riddles with your child. Have him or her name the fish from the story that answers each riddle. Then, work together to make up more fish riddles. (Turn the page to find the answers.)

1. I hide in the seaweed.
   I am as small as your knee.
   What am I?

2. I have a long nose.
   I may be 5 inches long.
   What am I?

 **School-Home Connection**

Invite your child to read *On the Bottom of the Sea* with you. Ask your child to name his or her favorite fish in the book.

| | |
|---|---|
| Word Count: | 235 |

| | |
|---|---|
| Vocabulary Words: | straight |
| | remember |
| | knee |

| | |
|---|---|
| Phonic Elements: | Long Vowel: /ē/*e, ea, ee* |
| | sea    keeps |
| | each    be |
| | we |
| | seaweed |

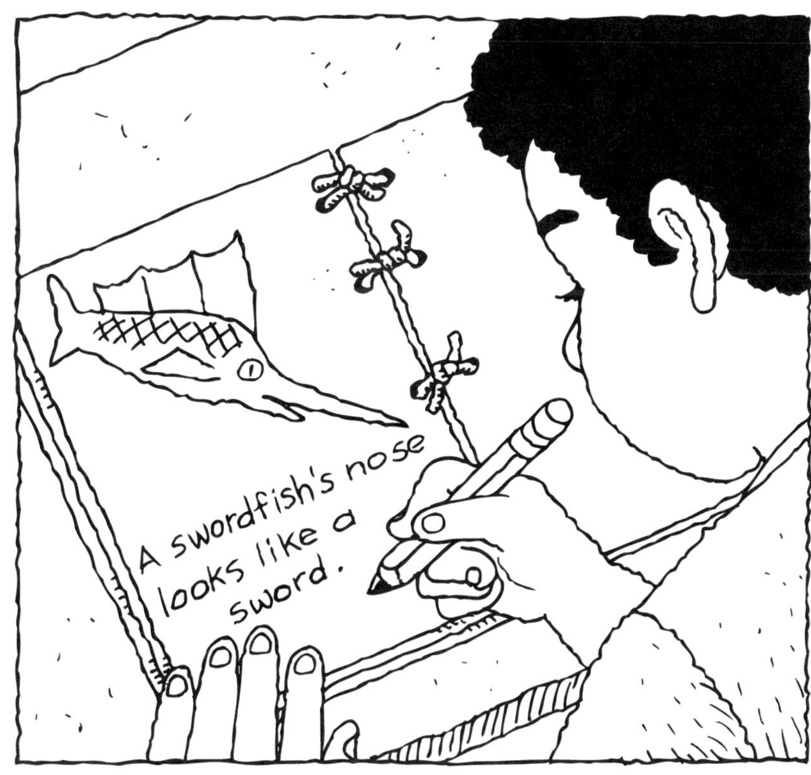


What are some fish you know? Make your own book, and draw some fish in it. Then write something you remember about each one.

**12**

These are butterfly fish. Why don't they look the same? It's because there are many kinds of butterfly fish!

**1**

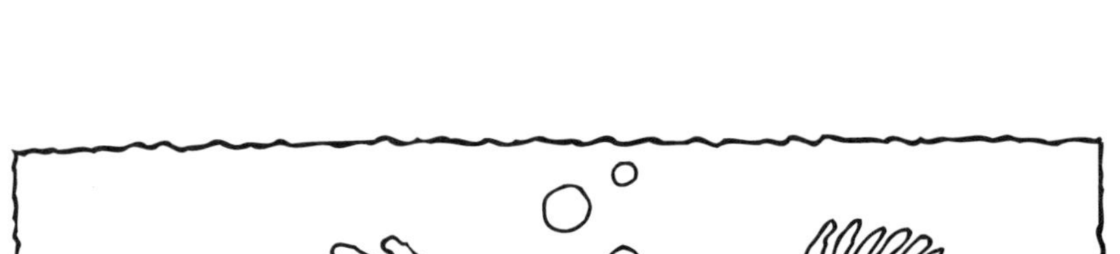

These are long-nosed butterfly fish. The black dot by the tail keeps larger fish away because the dot looks like a large eye.

**2**

Butterfly fish and sea horses both live in the sea. Other fish do, too. Some are big. Some are small. Some look like the names we give them!

**11**

Harcourt

These sea horses are going
straight through the seaweed.
They can hide there because
they look like the seaweed.

This is a butterfly fish, too. It
is called the lined butterfly fish.
How do you think it got that
name?

This butterfly fish has 16 lines.
The lines go straight down its
side.

4

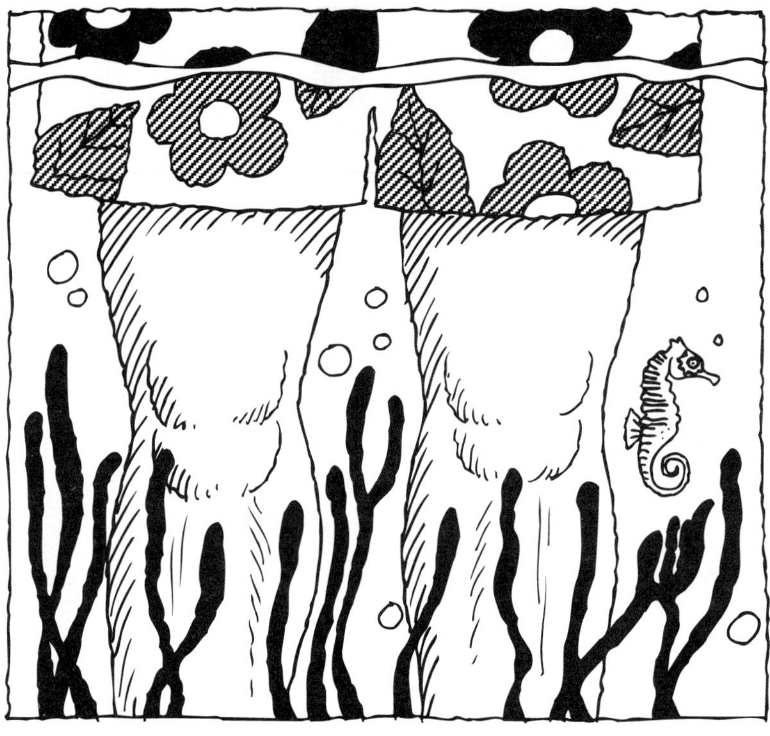

Most sea horses are small.
Some of the biggest sea horses
are about the size of your hand
or knee.

9

This is a sea horse. Some
people think that a sea horse
looks like a swimming horse.



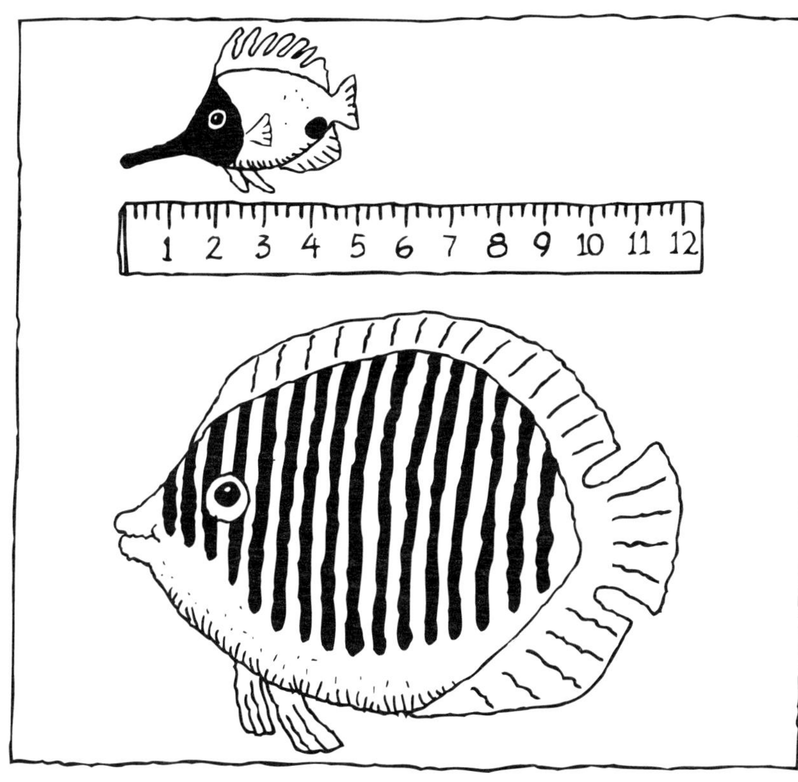



The long-nosed butterfly fish
is 5 inches long. The lined
butterfly fish is much longer.
It can be 12 inches long.

Most butterfly fish have bright colors, lines, or shapes on them. How do they look like butterflies?

**6**

Look at these fish. What do they look like to you?

**7**

Harcourt

TAKE-HOME BOOK
*Set Sail*
Use with "Baboon."

TIPTON ELEMENTARY PRIMARY

# Monkey Fun

**by Elizabeth Field**
**illustrated by Dave Blanchette**

## Teacher/Family Member ...........................................

### Monkey See, Monkey Do!
Remind your child that monkeys like to imitate the actions of others.
Then play a game together. Take turns pantomiming actions for each
other to mimic.

 **School-Home Connection**
Ask your child to read *Monkey Fun* to you. Help your child create new
pages for the book.

Word Count:            154

Vocabulary Words:      disappear
                       across
                       ground
                       mouth
                       shook

Phonic Elements:       Short Vowel: /e/*ea*
                       head
                       ahead

                       Long Vowel: /ī/*igh*
                       flight
                       night
                       high

Little monkey in a tree,
You shook your head at me.
Look ahead and all around.
Tell me what you see!

**12**

Little monkey in a tree,
Like a bird in flight,
You jump across the trees all day.
What do you do at night?

**1**

Little monkey in a tree,
Tell me what you hear.

**2**

You pop the fruit into your mouth.
Is it nice and sweet?

**11**

Harcourt

Little monkey in a tree,
You found fruit to eat.

10

Is it a bird or snake or cat?
Or just your mom who's near?

3

Little monkey in a tree,
Swinging by your tail,



Or do you like to stay up high?
What is that you've found?

Little monkey in a tree,
Jump down to the ground!

You swing from branch to branch.
Through the trees you sail!

Little monkey in a tree,
Did you disappear?

Or are you playing hide-and-seek
In the tree tops here?

6

7

Harcourt

TAKE-HOME BOOK
**Set Sail**
Use with "Planets."

Answers:  hear—rocket or spacecraft;    see—planets or comets;
touch —heat or cold;   smell—nice or like ice;   taste—green cheese

# Little Star

**by David Webb**
*illustrated by Claude Martinot*

## Teacher/Family Member .............................................

### Star Sense

The girl in the story asks about the five senses. Have your child draw a star on his or her paper and label each point with the name of one of the senses. Then have your child write one word to tell what the girl asks about that sense. (Turn the page to find the answers.)

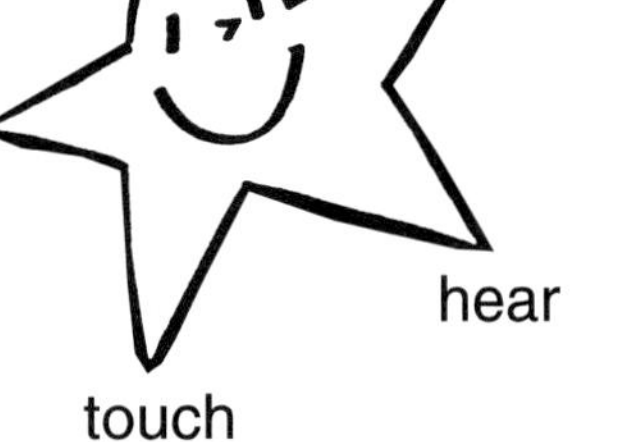

 **School-Home Connection**
Have your child read *Little Star* to you. Then ask your child to choose something else in space and to tell about space from that object's point of view.

Word Count:          165

Vocabulary Words:    rocket
                     spacecraft
                     planet
                     space
                     pictures

Phonics Element:     Long Vowel: $/\bar{a}/$ *a-e*
                     face
                     space
                     spacecraft
                     make

Harcourt

Twinkle, twinkle, little star,
I love you the way you are.
Little star with twinkling light,
Now I must sleep—Good night!

**12**

Twinkle, twinkle, little star,
What's it like up where
you are?
Help me, little shining face,
Picture how it is in space.

**1**

Twinkle, twinkle, little star,
Won't you tell me what
you hear?

Do you eat the moon's
green cheese?
Does the moon dust make
you sneeze?

Twinkle, twinkle, little star,
Won't you tell me what
you eat?

Do you hear the spacecraft fly?
Do the rockets soar on by?

Twinkle, twinkle, little star,
Won't you tell me what
you see?

Do you think that space
smells nice?
Or does it have no smell,
like ice?

Harcourt

Twinkle, twinkle, little star,
Won't you tell me what
you smell?



How do planets look to you?
Can you see some comets, too?

Twinkle, twinkle, little star,
Won't you tell me what
you feel?

Does Venus warm you with
its heat?
Does Pluto give you chilly feet?

6

7